God, Why Did You Wake Me?

God, Why Did You Wake Me?

Joane Cajuste

Copyright © 2017 Joane Cajuste
All rights reserved.

ISBN-13: 9781545448076
ISBN-10: 1545448078

Acknowledgement

Special Thanks to God, my creator, for helping me break the chains that bound me for so long.

I would like to express my love and gratitude to my mother, Chantal, for playing the role of both mom and dad in my life and for the sacrifices you made to make sure my needs were met.

To my amazing sister Tania who has been my biggest cheerleader. To my siblings Murielle, Jeffrey and Nadine for your support and encouragement.

To my first spiritual mentor, Donna, who first planted the seed to a better way of living. To my current spiritual mentor, Laura, who came into my life when I was at a crossroads and wanted to give up. You helped me build a better relationship with God.

To my wonderful friends Marlyse, Dafina, Mia, Raushanah, Edelyne, Abdiel, Lisa and to my cousin Daphne for your patience, understanding and love throughout the years. You all have shown me what a tribe truly is. You listened to my cries, frustration, confusion and have stood by me through my transformation, even during the ugly times.

To my business coach, Tiana, for your tough love, inspiration and guidance in writing this book.

To my honey, Tony, for the smile you put on my face and the butterflies I still get in my stomach when I'm around you. I'm lucky and grateful to be in a place where I'm able to appreciate and receive your love.

Table of Contents

	Acknowledgement · · · · · · · · · · · · · · · ·v	
Chapter 1	The Committee in my Head · · · · · · · · · · · · · · ·	1
Chapter 2	Nothing Left to Stand on, the Jig was Up · · · ·	9
Chapter 3	Finding Your Spiritual Connection · · · · · · · · ·	17
Chapter 4	Healing Old Wounds · · · · · · · · · · · · · · · · · ·	27
Chapter 5	Don't Hide, Don't Settle · · · · · · · · · · · · · · · ·	39
Chapter 6	Be Kind to Yourself · · · · · · · · · · · · · · · · · · ·	49
Chapter 7	A Disease of More ·	57
Chapter 8	The Inner Circle ·	67
Chapter 9	Being of Service ·	77

Chapter 10   It's not about them · · · · · · · · · · · · · · · · · · · 85

Conclusion · 95

"The Worst bullies you will ever encounter in your life are your own thoughts."
– BRYANT MCGILL

CHAPTER 1
The Committee in my Head

The mind is a powerful thing. Many of us have a hard time being kind to ourselves. We constantly beat ourselves up. Our thoughts can shape the way we view ourselves, life, and others. I believe that our thoughts are directly correlated to our happiness, peace, and success. It's no coincidence that what we think affects us physically as well. Negative thinking can bring about stress, tension, and depression throughout the body.

The whole purpose of negative thinking is to make you feel worse, and there's nothing to gain from it. In fact, negative thinking robs you of the chance to think positively, thereby preventing you from getting the benefits that come along with positive thinking. Imagine the things you could enjoy if you think positively: success, greater confidence, higher self-esteem, peace of mind, more energy, health benefits, and to crown it all, you live a more worthwhile life. Do not let your thoughts bully you out of enjoying all these.

I grew up in poverty in Brooklyn during the crack era. I was raised by a single mother who was doing the best she could raising her 5 children in a small one-bedroom apartment. I experienced various traumas as a little girl that snatched away my innocence and crushed my self-esteem. From being a fatherless child, to surviving sexual abuse as a little girl from the hands of two male adults, to spending some time in a foster home, I don't think it was much of a surprise when my life became destructive in adulthood. In fact, all my life had been building up to it. As a young adult, to escape the sadness and helplessness of my life, I drank, smoked, binged on food, partied daily and hung out with the wrong people. I didn't see the irony at the time that I was escaping a sad life by living a life that was destined to bring the same sadness and emptiness. All I knew was that life was a fog, and I had to push through it.

It wasn't until years later, as I approached thirty, that my life changed. I met God, and I was determined to clean up my life. I was done with the toxic habits that were crippling my life. I stopped drinking, smoking, and partying excessively, and I was working out more. I had a vision now. I started working on my career goals, eating well, and for the first time I felt I was truly living a life that had meaning.

And then I met what I call the committee: a negative force like an unexpected storm that seemed determined to uproot the life I was building, the life that God had given me and wanted for me.

The committee was made up of the negative critical voices in my head that suddenly reared its ugly head and wanted to sabotage everything that I was striving to achieve. The committee or voices in my head would meet daily to try and destroy me. The committee was powerful.

The day it began was like any other day. I can't recall the exact day, but I remember it being an early morning as I lay on my bed. I could see from my bedroom window as the sun rose slowly, its golden light seeping through the window. It would have been a beautiful morning except for the roaring negative thoughts in my head, telling me in myriad ways that I wasn't good enough. It said that whatever I was doing to change my life was useless and nothing would come of it. It was as though an unknown negative force was determined to keep me hostage in my own head, bullying me to surrender to its wishes. I couldn't escape it even if I wanted to, and I desperately wanted to.

The thoughts went over and over as I lay on that bed. My limbs were weak, and my soul was weary as I heard the committee in my head say the most spirit-draining things to me, and before I knew it, I was believing these strange unknown voices. These powerful voices that were determined to keep me down. And that day for the first time since I had turned my life around, I stopped my routine. I didn't go to the gym or do any form of exercise. I didn't think of my career that I was gradually building, I didn't think of friends, and I didn't remember to think of God. All I wanted to do was stay indoors, under the cover of my duvet, block out the sun, and mourn the sadness of my life. After all, the voices were telling me I wasn't worth anything, and I believed it wholeheartedly.

Perhaps I should have expected this day would come after all the traumatic events I had experienced. I couldn't help but wonder maybe this committee had been inside my head the whole time and I didn't notice because I drowned them in alcohol, food, cigarettes, and heavy partying.

But no amount of expectation could have prepared me for the emptiness the committee brought along with it that morning. And it was extremely painful to watch myself succumb to this because I had worked hard and was still working hard to get a better life. That day I tried to fight it, but with each try to beat it, the committee became louder and louder, as if pushing me to go back to my former ways or to even quit life as a whole. But I fought still, not succumbing to its suggestion to quit life or go back to my former ways. Even though it didn't look like it then, I had fought not to give in, at least totally.

After meeting the committee on that early morning, the committee became relentless. And soon, I began to notice a pattern. The committee seemed to exert its power more in the early morning before I opened my eyes or right before my feet hit the ground. And then I knew its purpose: it didn't want me to wake up, and if I did, it didn't want me to live. The committee's job was to make me feel worthless and to have me dead—spiritually, mentally, and emotionally.

Sometimes I'd have moments of reprieve, but like a cloud, it wasn't always far behind. Sometimes the committee in my head was so loud and unbearable that I would lay in bed right after waking up, staring at the ceiling with tears rolling down my eyes asking, **"God, why did you wake me?" Wishing he didn't**. The committee during that time in my life wanted me to stay in bed and would tell me things like, *Why bother getting up? What's the point? You are a failure, you haven't done much with your life. You've wasted a lot of time. You're too old to try x, y, and z. You have nothing to offer, and your dreams and goals are just a fantasy. Why don't you just give it up already?*

Some days I heard the committee louder than other days. I felt their presence in my chest, my stomach, and in my breathing. I wish I could tell you that I fought and won against this committee immediately. Or that I sent it packing before it did any damage, but that isn't true. The committee had the upper hand for many years in my life, and it showed through my actions and inactions. There were many career opportunities I passed up because I thought I wasn't good enough. I had relationships with friends, boyfriends, family members, and co-workers that I had nurtured while allowing myself to be taken advantage of, not standing up for myself. I didn't know my worth. The committee in my head wouldn't allow me to see my worth. I was constantly living in a place of fear and lack instead of abundance and trust. Most of all and the saddest of all, I was not living in the present. I was trapped in my mind and was living in the future or the past but never the present, and that's a painful place to be. To live life to the fullest, one has got to stay in the present, and the committee robbed me of that.

Although the committee is still there lurking in the shadows of my head, I am now more determined to fight it like a bully that it is. It now remains quiet more times than not. Some days, like the sneaky thing that it is, it will try to seep through any and all cracks to try to bring me down throughout the day. But I always search for the positive no matter what negative thing the committee is spewing. I tell myself I'm alive and that is a good thing no matter what the committee would have me believe. With each day, my feet hit the ground when I wake up, and I'm grateful because it's another opportunity to prove the committee wrong. Once my feet hit the ground, the committee begins to lose a lot of its power, and that counts. I starve it out of its negative and toxic power and focus on the positive no matter what the committee says in my head. Therein lies the power in fighting the committee.

Although the committee still on some days lurk around, I'm more than determined to fight it each day with the help of God by taking positive actions. A dear friend named Antwan once said that, "There are two pit bulls living inside all of us. One good and one bad. Each fighting to get on top." He was asked, "Which Pit bull wins?" His response was, "Whichever we feed the most."

I thank God that I've now been introduced to the committee because I know once the negative thoughts filter into my mind, they are not of God. I didn't know that, and I believed the voices to be true. The voice of God in me is now bigger than any other voice. It took me a lot of heartache, turmoil, pain, and sadness to finally find the answers and quiet the committee. Right now, my hope is to share my story and help those who are struggling to have a loving relationship with themselves, those selling themselves short, or just trudging through life, getting their butt kicked by their internal demons, living in the past or living an unfulfilled life to find their magnificence, their power, and remember that they are worthy of an extraordinary life.

A great tool I use when negative thinking tries to bully its way through is to ask myself if what I'm thinking at that moment serves me and makes me feel good. That's always my first step. I try not to judge myself for having negative thoughts, and I try not to beat myself up. A friend once told me if I'm adamant about beating myself up for negative thinking, then I should beat myself up with a feather. What you think, you will become. If you think you are great, then you will live a life mostly of greatness, but if you think you're inadequate, then you will live a life that doesn't feel like it's worth living. You may not be able to control the negative thoughts that enter your mind. But you have the choice to make a conscious decision to feed your mind positivity and light.

Eventually the positivity and light will crowd out the darkness. There will be little room left for the negativity to live in, but it will take work, and you must be vigilant. The work will not be easy, but it will be worth it.

"Rock bottom became the solid foundation on which I rebuilt my life."
— J.K. Rowling

CHAPTER 2
Nothing Left to Stand on, the Jig was Up

Many of us have to hit a brick wall, with nowhere to turn, and feel defeated before the magic happens. This holds true when it comes to breaking bad habits. Sometimes we're not aware of the damage being done when we're engaging in these bad habits but eventually, we slowly become aware, and it's not until the pain of those habits kicks in and becomes intolerable that we're willing to seek change. Sometimes we have to hit rock bottom before we can crawl out of the hell we're in. Humans are stubborn; we will cling to something knowing it doesn't serve us just because it brings temporary joy or relief, and then we hope that we won't suffer the same consequences as others who have gone through this path. But then we soon find out that we're no different, and eventually the pain of repeating the same habits becomes so demoralizing that we are forced to start afresh, get a new plan and rebuild. Hitting rock bottom was probably the best thing that ever happened to me.

I don't think there is a human being on earth who doesn't have a demon they will soon encounter or already encountered. The demon can be obvious or it can be very subtle. Demons can range from trying to keep up with the Joneses knowing you're in major debt to procrastination, shopping excessively, overeating, bingeing, gossiping, envy, lust, greed, tearing people down to make yourself feel better, sleeping with married or unavailable people, sleeping around, abusing others, alcohol abuse, drugs, and stealing. The list is endless. But know that a demon is anything that you are participating in that keeps you from becoming your best self.

My own personal demon was that I never wanted to feel negative emotions whether it was sadness, frustration, anger, guilt, fear, doubt, envy, shame, regret, despair, etc. I always wanted to be on a high. And there was no better way than to escape with a glass of wine or a glass of Hennessey or maybe a shot of tequila chased by a Corona after a hard day at work or right before a party. Another great escape was food. I absolutely loved and enjoyed food, and I never deprived myself of the occasional treat or junk food. Having a cigarette in my hand, preferably a Newport cigarette, was the icing on the cake. Of course, I knew that cigarettes were an ugly and obvious demon that I had to let go of, but the alcohol and food abuse crept up on me. These habits helped to take the edge off—that not-quite-right-but-can't-put-your-finger-on-it type of feeling. Feeling as if something is missing, a chronic irritability or discomfort. But the problem with curbing any kind of unwanted feelings or emotions with your demon of choice is that the effect will eventually wear out, and you will have no choice but to keep replenishing that demon, and on and on it will go till you can't pick yourself back up.

Unfortunately, at the time, these crutches seemed like the only coping mechanisms I had to make me feel good when I was down. I didn't know how else to fill that hole inside of me. I had no other tools to help me with the sadness, emptiness or the overwhelming feelings that would rise up when I thought about some of my childhood trauma that would subtly haunt me from time to time, or when I thought about my struggling financial situation, or when I had to face some serious health concerns, or when I thought about my absent father. The list went on. I used these crutches hoping they would give me some sort of peace, and at times they appeared to have given me some peace.

That's the tricky thing about demons or unhealthy coping mechanisms: they appear to work at the beginning. You feel like you can manage them, like you have control. They make you feel elated and even satisfied. They trick you into believing the empty void in your life is being filled. But that false sense of peace I thought I felt was just a lie. In the end, I was left with the same issues but now had to also suffer the consequences of my personal demons.

When I realized what MY own demons were, it was like waking up from a trance and suddenly realizing that you are in the boxing ring with a heavyweight champion like Mike Tyson or Muhammed Ali. Here you are, against a ring, nowhere to move and you are getting knocked out by this powerful thing. It would require an absolute miracle to win.

My excessive drinking, smoking, and eating took a toll on my body, my mind, my spirit, and my relationships with friends, family, and loved ones. I wasn't able to fully show up for others. I became isolated from those who loved me. The excess food, alcohol, and cigarettes made me feel sluggish, constantly bloated, and physically horrible. The demons robbed me of my ambition, I made foolish choices when it came to the men I dated, and I put myself in compromising situations. I became complacent with life. Any fears I had about any situation were magnified. I felt horrible but didn't know how to stop, didn't know if I could stop and sometimes just didn't care to stop. I stopped caring about myself, people, and important things. There was no more urgency in anything for me.

However, the day I hit rock bottom was like any other day for me: blurry and fatigued. I had passed out on my couch not knowing how I got there or what time it was when the TV woke me up. I squinted at the images that flickered like a blur on the TV not making sense of it, until finally, one stuck.

I remember that face, beautiful and young. It was the face of a woman who seemed to have big things ahead of her. And yet, the voice on the TV was saying she had committed suicide. I don't know why, but that voice trickled down my spine as if the coldest of waters was being poured on me. It jolted me out of my own blurry state, and as I turned the TV off, I said to myself, "I can absolutely see why someone would commit suicide; at least her pain is gone." And then I burst into uncontrollable, heart-wrenching tears. It was as if I was mourning this stranger that I didn't know but was somehow connected to me. Like I was exposed to a glimpse of the pain she experienced before taking her life. I had never been close to committing suicide, but I was at the place where I didn't want to quite die but didn't want to live either.

That night, I could do nothing but cry, for her and for me. I cried till I was exhausted. I cried till it became clear that something had to change. This was my rock bottom moment—the moment death tried to dance with me.

Rock bottoms are eye openers. They are the place where you get to, and you realize that your present demons or bad habits cannot sustain you. It's the moment you realize that the jig is up. It was at this point that I finally admitted to myself that there was not enough alcohol, food, cigarettes, partying, television or sleeping that could fill the hole inside of me, numb me or bring any kind of joy in my life. It was the moment I was forced to start rebuilding my life.

It was after that night that I was able to confide in a close friend about the feelings I was having and about some of my addictive behaviors and terrible vices. The next step was to seek help from a therapist and from free support groups for my drinking, smoking, horrible relationship with food and the sexual abuse I had experienced as a little girl. I was in my twenties when I finally discovered the power of therapy. My 5-year-old self still carried shame and guilt from having been violated by two separate men who were supposed to be friends of the family. I couldn't heal on my own. I also couldn't push away or ignore the pain anymore. It wasn't until I fully committed to healing my life that I realized those experiences were still subconsciously buried in me. I told myself that I was an adult and everything was okay now, but that was a lie. Deep down, I was still an afraid 5-year-old girl who was also hurt, angry, sad, anxious, and fearful. I felt filthy, walked around with my head down and was crying to be rescued. I needed to get the help required to be set free. I had to let the little girl inside of me know she was no longer alone. I had to tell her, *Baby girl, I hear you and I'm here for you.*

I believed in the idea of God, but I didn't quite have a true relationship with God. However, I did start seeking spiritual food in the form of spirituality books from different authors. I would dust off my Bible and read Psalms from time to time. Sometimes I didn't understand what I was reading, but I clung to the passages that uplifted and moved me. I followed spiritual gurus on TV or in the media. At the time, those were things that gave me a glimmer of sanity. I also had at least 1 or 2 people I could be open and honest with as I tried to get rid of the demons and poison in my life. I can't stress how important it is to find at least one trustworthy person you can lean on in moments of uncertainty and temptation. Our demon's best weapon is when we keep ourselves in isolation.

The above steps were the process that helped me scratch the surface when it came to healing and rebuilding. The process of rebuilding is not easy, sometimes we must hit rock bottom first. The most important thing rock bottoms do for us is to force us to look in the mirror, realize that the jig is up, and admit to ourselves that the demons do not serve us, no matter how tricky they are. Rock bottoms force us to be honest with ourselves and admit that we do not have as much control as we thought we did. And as the quote above said, rock bottoms become the honest, solid foundation we can begin to rebuild the life we truly deserve and the life God wants for us.

CHAPTER 2 NOTES

- **What are some of the things holding you back?** These can be subtle things that keep you from thriving and being your very best physically, mentally, spiritually and emotionally. They may even appear to bring you temporary relief and feel good, but in the long run, they may be doing more damage than good.

Examples: Procrastination, substance abuse, gossip, negative self-talk, jealousy, smoking, excessive drinking, excessive eating, inappropriate and toxic relationships, etc. Don't judge yourself when jotting these down. The point of this exercise is to simply bring awareness.

_____

_____

_____

_____

_____

_____

_____

_____

_____

"You will seek me and find me, when you seek me with all your heart."
- JEREMIAH 29:13

CHAPTER 3
Finding Your Spiritual Connection

Religion is the commitment or devotion to a religious faith while spirituality is the sense of connection to something bigger than ourselves. Most times religion can serve as an avenue to explore our spirituality, but spirituality is not limited to that. Spirituality involves a search for meaning in life. It involves asking the question, "Why am I here?" Every one of us asks this question at one point or the other. We live in a world where things happen to us, and we want to know why and if there is a sense to it or meaning in anything.

We want to believe that things just don't happen to us at random, and so we seek connection to an entity bigger than ourselves. Some may find that their spiritual life is connected to churches or a religious gathering, while for others it involves having a personal connection with God, a higher power or nature. But one thing is for certain, we all have a need deep down in us to be connected to something more than just the physical world. And when we truly seek for that interconnectedness to something bigger than us, it is then we will find our deep sense of purpose and our reason for being.

For a major part of my life, I was running the show. I was the captain of my ship. I did the best I could with the tools I had in the quest of living a fulfilled life. But even as much as I tried, there was always a gaping hole, a feeling that something was missing in my life, that no matter how hard I tried to fill it up, it still felt inadequate.

Everything I tried to give me peace and happiness wasn't working. The overall irritability, discontent, fear, worry, anxiety, and insecurity still played a huge part in my life more than I thought it would, even after I started to get rid of the destructive behaviors that caused me pain. As much as I tried every day to be grateful, it was hard. I was alive, but I wasn't quite living. The fulfillment that I sought after still eluded me, and I knew I needed to find something bigger than me that would lift me up, but I didn't exactly know what the answer was. However, it was at this crossroad of my life that I started to meet people who were either really religious, had a relationship with God or followed some sort of spiritual practice. But I was skeptical about religion being the answer.

I wasn't unfamiliar with religion; in fact, I grew up fairly religious. I was baptized as a young girl and did my communion in the Catholic Church. I grew up in a family that believed in God, read the Bible, and prayed from time to time, so the idea of God and praying weren't foreign to me, even though I never truly understood the ritual of prayer or who God was. I just followed the rules I was given as a little girl, and that seemed enough. But as I grew older, I became extremely judgmental and critical of religion. I had heard of tales of bad and horrible things that went on in some churches and with some religious leaders, and I let that deter me from learning more about God and religion.

It was as if there was a universal orchestration at this juncture in my life because everything I knew was pointing me to take a second look at religion even though I was skeptical about it. For one, I was getting desperate to fill the inescapable gaping hole in my life, and then almost everyone I knew seemed to be finding their own spiritual connections and were discussing their relationships with God.

One of those people was my very good friend Jackie, whom I met in college. I remember she came around one summer afternoon after I had begun to feel that something was missing in my life. I hadn't told her this of course, and then out of nowhere, she blurted out that she had made a decision to become a Jehovah's Witness. It took a second before that registered in, and my eyes grew wide when it did. I couldn't believe it. This was a girlfriend I had partied hard with. We had always been more concerned with looking good, having fun, drinking, smoking, going to the clubs and meeting cute guys, and we had hardly ever discussed religion or God. It really was never a priority.

But here she was, telling me about her faith and about her willingness to know more. At first, I thought it was because of her new boyfriend who was a Jehovah's Witness and the person who introduced her to the faith, but the excitement with which she began to tell me about it made me know it was something more. A light sparkled in her eyes and her smiled widened across her face; she felt almost alien to me. It was what I imagined peace and happiness to look like and for a second as I watched her, I was jealous.

She too felt that something was missing in her life when she had made this decision. She started attending services at their place of worship called Kingdom Hall, and I could see that she genuinely liked it. I, the skeptic, began to see the transformation for myself. She was partying less, she talked about God more, she talked less of men and getting money but more of love for humanity and how she could make a difference in the world. I was amazed by her transformation. She was still the same sweet friend I knew, but happier, more content, and more grounded. And a few years later, she made the decision to get baptized and become a Jehovah's Witness.

Watching this transformation unfold right before my eyes made me put my sentiments about religion aside, and I decided to learn more about my friend's religious path. I went to a few services with her, read Jehovah's Witness materials and their Bible. What got me every time I visited was the warmth and kindness with which Jackie and the members of her congregation always welcomed me. Their genuine happiness and their sense of purpose were so contagious that it illuminated my own desire to search for mine. I began to delve deeper into other forms of religions: Seventh-Day Adventist, Baptist, Methodist, and Buddhism.

Things started to shift as I began to explore the idea of what it would mean to rely on God truly. I knew I was on the right path because I started to actually feel that something bigger than me was taking care of me. I started to feel better as I began to know more of this thing called God. My outlook became more positive. There was an increasingly warm and fuzzy feeling inside of me that there was little room for doubt. I thought to myself, *whether God is real or not, I don't want these feelings to go away.*

However, I knew that committing to a specific religion wasn't the thing for me and wasn't the path for me at that time, so I made a decision to turn my life to God as I understood God. Meaning, I had to have my own relationship with God and define my God. I knew in my heart that I couldn't just rely on religion to define who God was to me. I was no longer praying to God, but my prayers were now talks and chats with a best friend. My *best friend, God, Higher Power or Father*, all names I have for this big spiritual, magical power that has my back. The God I now know loves me unconditionally. The God I have come to know is LOVE. The God I know doesn't discriminate against anyone no matter their religion, background, gender, or sexual orientation. The God I know is an all-inclusive God. The God I know wants me to be happy, joyous, and free.

When I look back at the life I had prior to developing a relationship with God, I realize that God was probably with me all along. There were many situations I put myself into that should've destroyed me or had me dead, but when I decided to seek a spiritual life eagerly, my God was revealed to me.

It's important for me to nourish my spirit, and I do so through spiritual practices. A few of my spiritual practices consist of a few minutes of daily meditation in the morning right before I leave the house. Meditation helps me hear what God is saying. Not in the physical sense but the spiritual sense. I hear my God the loudest when I'm still, and this is shown by my actions throughout my day. I'm less impulsive. I'm more fearless, confident, patient, loving and understanding. I make better decisions throughout the day when I can meditate, even if it is just for 5 minutes in the morning, and if for some reason I forget in the morning, I can take 5 minutes to meditate any time during the day. I don't think there is a right or wrong way to meditate. There are so many forms of meditation to choose from.

Journaling my thoughts and feelings without any judgment is also another of my favorite spiritual practices. There is something very therapeutic about expressing your feelings on paper. I also do a lot of conscious deep breathing throughout the day. Even if for just a few seconds to a minute at a time. And I read spiritual materials, including the Bible. Lastly, I chat with God or what most people would call praying to God. There are days I use every tool in my toolbox and some days I just practice two or three.

When I follow my spiritual practices, I feel like I'm being led and directed each step of the way during the day. I don't get frazzled. My mind is not constantly racing. I know for sure these behaviors are not of me but of my God, something bigger than me because I was definitely NOT the kind of person yesterday that I am today. Not by a long shot. My understanding for others has improved greatly. I'm learning every day to love and to treat people the way my God loves and treats me. My compassion for others has increased, but more importantly, the compassion I have gained for myself is priceless. I feel like I'm being taken care of. I'm learning more about God's role in my life every day.

Most days, I feel so content and fulfilled that sometimes my ONLY prayer for the day is, THANK YOU. These, of course, are my own methods, and I have to make it clear that it is important that we all find a spiritual path that resonates with us. If this resonates with you, awesome! But if not, find one that guides you, one that makes you feel better about yourself and humanity at large. A spiritual connection that keeps you grounded and makes you feel alive and less alone in this world. Something that reminds you that there is more to life than the physical and material world. You deserve that, and you need to find that path for yourself.

CHAPTER 3 NOTES

Perhaps you already have your own spiritual practice and beliefs but haven't been in touch with them for a while. Maybe you are still searching to find a spiritual path that resonates with your heart and soul. I think it's important for us to believe in something bigger than ourselves, even if this means we can't see or touch it—a belief that something is taking care of us at all times.

- **What does it mean to believe that something or some power is taking care of YOU at all times?** Whether you are spiritual, religious, still searching, confused or skeptical, let's reflect or imagine for a moment what this would look like in your life. How would this belief manifest in your attitude, relationships, outlook, career, love life, self-esteem, etc.?

I call my power, God. If you can't define what that power is for you right now, that is perfectly fine. Just imagine that there is a power bigger than you that wants you to WIN.

_____

_____

_____

_____

_____

"Don't allow your wounds to turn you into a person you are not."
– PAULO COELHO

CHAPTER 4
Healing Old Wounds

Sometimes, in order to continue to move towards the vision we have for our life, we have to pull the curtains back on our past and look at some of the issues and circumstances that have brought us agony, stress or sorrow. Some wounds need to be addressed in order for us to become the person we are truly meant to be. This can be a painful process, but it's impossible to live the life we deserve if we are consciously or subconsciously making decisions and living from a wounded place.

To let go of the past and its baggage, we have to confront it, understand why things went the way they did, and sometimes realize that it wasn't our fault and forgive ourselves and others that may have wronged us. Until we bravely look our past in the face, we will never realize the full potential we are capable of or find the happiness we so desire.

I was a few days shy of 11 on that warm spring evening. I was at home with my mother and my other siblings. I remember us gathering in front of the TV, my little brother sitting close to my mom and laughing at a scene on the *Cosby Show*, while my sisters sat attentively, as did I. *The Cosby Show* was a staple in almost everyone's home, especially in the homes of African-American families back then, and none of us could afford to miss any of it.

And then there was a sudden loud knock at the door, interrupting the show. My mother patted my brother's head before she stood up to open the door. While I and the rest of my siblings were still rooted in front of the TV, my mother was being greeted by two policemen and a woman who identified herself as a social worker. Our attention was torn from the TV when we heard the cops tell my mom that they had a reason to believe that my siblings and I were living in a dangerous and unfit environment and that my mother was an immediate threat and danger to us.

Confusion and disbelief clouded my mother's face then, while my siblings and I simply thought this was a prank. But then the social worker came around to our side and said they had been mandated by the courts to take all three of us away and put us in temporary foster homes that night, and that made us panic. We had no clue what she was talking about; we thought maybe they had the wrong house.

I looked into my mother's face, waiting for her to clear things up, to tell them that we were fine, we may not have enough, but we were not facing any immediate threat or danger from my mother. Instead, I saw her own helplessness as she begged the policemen and social workers, with tears streaming down her face, demanding an explanation, while also pleading with them not to take her babies away.

It was days later that we would find some clarity to this absurdity, and even that was hard to believe. We learned that a trusted close relative that my mother loved dearly had concocted a vicious plan. The plan involved fabricated charges of neglect and harm brought against my mother in hopes of having NY State take my siblings and me away from my mother and have us live with her, for one reason only: MONEY. If my mother went to court and a jury found her guilty, then this so-called "loving relative" would be awarded custody of us and would get a monthly allowance to take care of us.

For a measly few hundred dollars a month, my mother experienced the worst betrayal and heartache any mother could experience. She was blind-sided. The heartache of having her kids snatched away from her and the betrayal from a family member was crushing. But my mother didn't let that deter her; she was ready to fight. I don't think I've ever seen my mother pray harder than she did during that time. She was able to pool her resources together by asking a few people she knew to help her get a lawyer.

Pending the trial, my siblings and I remained in foster homes. At that time, I was in a constant state of fear, worry, and panic (feelings that would unfortunately become very familiar in my later years). I thought I would never get to see my mom again. I was on pins and needles not knowing what to expect. I spent time looking over my shoulders and anticipating the worst while we were in our temporary foster homes, all the while hoping all would soon be over and I would go back to living with my mother and siblings.

When the day of the trial finally came, I was anxious. We knew the court verdict could go either way, and the thought of never living in the same home with my mother and siblings again was paralyzing. However, my anxiety was lifted when some hours to the trial, someone who knew about the malicious and vicious lies against my mother came forward and exposed this relative. After a thorough investigation, the justice system realized they didn't have a case; they had made a big mistake and the charges were dropped. Of course, this was great. We were back home, but unfortunately, the emotional damage of being torn from my mother and having to live in a foster home for a period of time was already done.

We were never the trusting, carefree kids we were any more (I for one went on to become the person who went through life always waiting for the other shoe to drop, not trusting too many people, never feeling safe and comfortable in my own skin, never feeling grounded) and neither was my mother.

I didn't meet my father until I was in my thirties. I don't have the same father as my other siblings, and growing up, I always imagined what he would be like. Would he look like me? I wondered which of his traits I had. Anything I couldn't explain from my mother's characteristics, I passed on to him. He dwelled in my fantasy, and he was perfect.

Well, until one day when I got the news that he was coming from Haiti and visiting NY for a weekend and he wanted to meet me. My whole body felt heavy, and my stomach felt queasy at the news. I was so nervous and scared. What if he didn't like me? What if it didn't go well? I was an adult, yet I was concerned about impressing this man that I'd never met.

But my heart was also open; I was excited at the opportunity to finally meet my father for the first time.

It was summer on a Saturday that I finally got my lifelong wish. When I saw him, all the nerves and the fear fell away, because in him, I saw myself. There was a striking resemblance. Had I met him on the street, I'd have stopped him and asked if we were related. He felt that familiar. We had the same nose, the same dark chocolate complexion, and some of the same quirky mannerisms.

It was at his sister's house in Long Island, NY that we met. We spent the whole day together with his side of the family present. It would also be my first time meeting his sister and the other relatives on my father's side. He was introducing me to everyone in his family, and I was welcomed with open arms. That day, I felt like a star, like I was important to this person who was a part of me and I had been waiting my whole life to meet.

By the time evening crept up on us, it was time for us to part ways. I didn't want it to end, but he assured me that he wanted to see me the following day and had plans for us to hang out, this time just the two of us. I was joyful and felt like a little school girl. For a moment, I understood what it might feel like to be a daddy's girl. The next day came, and I called my father to follow up on when and where we would meet. He said that something came up, and he wouldn't be able to meet after all, but next time he visited NY, we would hang out. My heart sank at hearing that. It sounded like a lame excuse to me.

What could be more important than spending time with the daughter you've never known? The daughter you finally had a chance to meet after 30-something plus years? I was devastated and heartbroken; the feelings I had the first time I met him were undone by this rejection. For whatever reason, I wasn't his priority. I would never get to the answers I wanted, like why didn't he make an attempt to have a relationship with me all these years? Why was he loyal and a great father to the other two kids he had by another woman who wasn't my mom?

I haven't seen my father since and probably can count the number of times we've spoken over the phone on one hand. And sometimes I wonder if things had been better between us, if I had grown up with him present, if he had cared about me enough, maybe then at that time I would've been more comfortable with being in a committed relationship with a man.

At that time in my life, I could never give my heart to a man. I was always more comfortable in having a sexual relationship with a man with no strings attached, but any talk of commitment was a deal breaker for me. I just couldn't risk the blow of having someone else abandon me, so it was much easier to build a wall. Truthfully, the thought of a man being able to sustain a loving relationship was foreign to me and not doable.

It wasn't until my thirties after meeting my father that I was able to embark on my first committed relationship. Going through life not giving people a chance and blaming them for what my father did was no longer serving me. For me, to make the transition from being critical and cynical of men, I had to find my own closure. I had to accept the fact that my father was never the father he should've been or the father I wanted him to be. He had his own issues and would have to face his own mirror.

It came down to two choices for me: I could accept him for who he was or just move on and erase him from my heart and memory. I chose acceptance around the circumstances involving my dad, and I also chose to pray for him all the time.

I used to think that going back and dissecting some of my old wounds or past hurts was pointless. My attitude was that the past is the past and it should be left in the past. I thought to myself that what I went through didn't really matter because there were people who went through worse and they seemed perfectly fine. What I failed to realize was that I'm not them and they're not me. Yes, surviving a battle and coming through on the other side will make you stronger, but it's not enough to just survive.

I no longer wanted to live life in survival mode all the time. I wanted a life of optimism, looking at the glass half full, I wanted to walk around with an open heart, I wanted to feel grounded and feel like the universe had my back and that people weren't always out to get me or that people always had an agenda. I wanted to trust again. This meant I had to go beyond just surviving. I had to heal the old wounds that prevented me from being the woman I wanted to be, and that meant looking at the details of my life that shaped the woman I had become.

The first step was acceptance. Accepting that the past cannot be changed. The second step was doing away with the blame game. It was no longer acceptable for me to use the past or anyone in my past as a crutch to hang on to negativity. The third step for me was envisioning the type of woman I wanted to be. What was my ideal self? How did my ideal self think and act? The fourth step for me was seeking therapy to work through some of my past issues. Therapy may not be for everyone, but seeking guidance from a therapist, a professional or some kind of spiritual advisor or mentor is paramount. You want to be able to confide in someone who can help in the healing process, free of judgments. Someone you feel safe with. I don't believe we're put on earth to do the work alone.

The things I've been through in my past gave me the thick skin I have, but facing my past and attempting to make peace with the past made me stronger and more courageous, and it softened my heart and spirit.

CHAPTER 4 NOTES

Addressing and healing old wounds was just one of the keys I used to unlock the door to personal freedom. Many will need to seek outside help in the form of therapy or counseling to address certain wounds that have caused pain and trauma. These wounds may have affected us physically, mentally, spiritually and emotionally. Seeking outside help when necessary is not only courageous but the greatest act of kindness and love that one can show to themselves. There is no wound or pain too big or too small to address.

- **What in your life from the past or present still needs healing?**

  _____

  _____

  _____

  _____

  _____

  _____

- **Imagine the person you would be if you finally found freedom and peace around these wounds.** How would your body physically feel? How would your outlook improve? How would your confidence improve? How would your decision-making in important areas of your life improve? How would your relationships with others improve?

_____

_____

_____

_____

_____

"There is no passion to be found in playing small, in settling for a life that is less than the one you are capable of living."
— NELSON MANDELA

CHAPTER 5
Don't Hide, Don't Settle

I think the biggest disservice we can do to ourselves and others is not taking risks and going after our dreams. No matter how big, small or unrealistic the dream may seem, we have a right to experiment, to try new things, and to follow our heart. Many of us are too scared to jump and take the leap required to follow our dreams, and this is understandable because it's so much easier to play it safe. As human beings, we all have the strong desire to be loved, respected, but most of all, accepted. And that's what makes going after our dreams scarier.

When you're following your dreams and possibly going outside of the norm, you risk being vulnerable, exposed, and scrutinized, and you may actually fail. Most and I dare to say all people want to be liked. Living a life that is passionate and fulfilling will definitely bring about people that don't care or support what you are doing and even dislike you. But what's the alternative? Living a life that we're not meant to live? Pretending we're whole and happy? Being complacent, wandering through life with that gnawing feeling that you are meant for greatness but you've chosen to hide instead? Don't let this happen. Don't settle.

I've had a love for acting and theater since I was five. I played one of the orphans in the play *Annie* in the second grade, and I was told I stole the show. The following year I got the lead role in a play. I've forgotten the name of the play, but I played a vagrant who had many comedic lines and punch lines. I remember feeling good and received such great feedback. I would play dress up and create little skits at home with my cousins. I even put on mini shows for family members. These are one of the few times in my childhood I remember being free, happy, ecstatic, and comfortable in my own skin. I felt important and fearless when I played dress up and acted. After my lead role in elementary school, I didn't try my hand at acting until I was in college and took an intro to acting course to fulfill some of my liberal arts requirements. Once again, I was in my element and aced the class. I remember after the course was over, the teacher pulled me aside and told me that I really should give acting a shot and that I was great. It was good to get that validation, but I quickly disregarded his suggestion and continued on my path of working towards my bachelor's in biology. Biology seemed more logical; after all, I was told that it would be great if I tried my hands at becoming a doctor.

With a Caribbean family who values education and careers such as teaching, law or medicine, there was never any talk in pursuing careers outside of that. Definitely not acting. I went on to get my bachelor's in biology but knew there was no way medical school was for me. I continued to go from job to job and industry to industry "finding myself." I worked hard at every job I had. I pride myself on being a great employee. But I couldn't figure out why I would get so bored with a job and not last more than two years or so. If I didn't resign, somehow my position was terminated because of budget or relocation reasons. In hindsight, it became clear that these were all signs and whispers from God that the career and job paths I was pursuing were only temporary and would one day lead me to what I was intended to do.

In my late twenties, I met a girlfriend of mine named Leonore. With her friendship, the thought of acting came knocking again. Leonore was around the same age as me. She had a background in corporate America, and I distinctly remember the day she said she always wanted to be an actress and that she wanted to try her hand at auditioning for the first time in her life. My eyes lit up like a little school girl at the news, and I felt like I had found a kindred spirit. I thought her desire to try her hand at acting was so cool. So I told her I too once had a desire to act, but never pursued it, and just like that, we became a duo of aspiring actresses! We decided to look for auditions through *Backstage*—a popular newspaper for actors to find credible auditions. We went on to audition for community theater and independent movies. I landed a few background roles in movies and small bit theater parts. I then decided to take the leap and sign up for an acting class.

I was scared out of my mind the very first day I stepped into that class. Here I was in a class with seasoned and trained actors—people who had current roles on television, acted in blockbuster films, went to Julliard and NYU drama school, and all I had was my experience in my *Annie* play, my lead role in elementary school, and one intro class I took in college. But I soon found out it didn't matter. The timing was right, and that gnawing feeling of wanting to try something that I was too fearful to try wouldn't go away, so I had no choice but to follow my instincts. And the funniest thing happened. Despite being in a class with professional and seasoned actors, I did amazingly well, at least that's what I was told by my acting teacher and the students in the class.

That gnawing feeling slowly dissipated. I felt lighter. Still scared but lighter. Scared because I was worried what people would think of me. The story I fabricated in my head was that people would look at me like I had three heads when I told them that I wanted to become an actress in my late twenties. I was scared that I would look stupid, because although I had many supporters, I also heard the following, "Why would you go after a shaky and unpredictable career such as acting?" "You're a bit too old to get into that field." "Girl, that shipped may have passed." "You already have a college degree that you should be putting to use." "Pursuing this passion is costly, and you're already living paycheck to paycheck." All these opinions weighed on me, and the thought of what if they were right occurred to me, but bigger than all those opinions was the desire to go after my goals.

Feeling insecure about the whole process and unsure if I was doing the right thing, I went on to do it anyway. I went on to build my acting resume and got a few cool gigs and gained some great experience. I took the risk despite being scared. I put in overtime at work and used the extra income towards my craft. I cut unnecessary expenses. I sought out discounted and free events pertaining to studying the craft. I made sure to connect with the people on the same path. I made it happen. The result of not playing it safe or hiding or staying in my comfort zone made me feel electric and alive. I was so grateful that I was also able to share my gift with others.

The result of me not playing it safe meant that I was able to make an impact on other people's lives by bringing them joy through my craft. I thank God for introducing me to Leonore. Had God not placed this angel in my life, I may not have dared to take the risk and try. God brings exactly the right people and situation in your life at exactly the right time. Since then, I've gone on to explore many different passions of mine because I refuse to settle for less than I'm capable of. I'm a multi-passionate person who's in love with the arts, wellness, nutrition, and fitness. I'm open to all the beautiful possibilities waiting for me.

Not playing small is by no means an easy task. It means you have to make sacrifices, which can possibly affect your finances, time, family life, social life, people who may not support you, etc. But when you get uncomfortable enough, you will have no choice but to follow your dreams. As challenging as it may seem, God will place the right circumstances, tools, outlets, and opportunities to carry you along; you just have to take the first step and decide that you want something different for yourself and then devise a plan to get it. Don't rob yourself of not pursuing your goals and don't rob others of the positive impact they may experience as a result of you living your goals or dreams.

I don't want to settle for a life that isn't mine. I'm ready to take risks, even if it means I change my mind down the line or fall on my face and get back up. The alternative of not going after my dreams and goals is too painful. There is a price to pay when you don't follow your heart and go after your truth or when you hide. For me, I can always tell when I'm not being authentic, not working towards my dreams or living a lie. That lie manifests itself in many ways, such as: resentment, irritability, anger, judgments, sadness, eating too much, cynicism, sarcasm, and even rage. For a long time, the biggest thing I struggled with was caring what others thought and fear of failure. I still struggle with that. The difference between before and now is that I'm willing to walk through the discomfort, fear, and scrutiny anyway. Besides, people talk, so what. We're no better than or less than anyone else. I would like to think that me chasing my dreams and putting myself out there is not the biggest topic at anyone's dinner table. My mentor told me not to be arrogant enough to think people are always talking or concerned about what I'm doing. It's borderline narcissistic, and she's right. God did not make a mediocre or average woman. I am worthy, deserving, and meant to live a life beyond my wildest dreams. Note that wildest dreams do not equate to the magnitude of the dream. It doesn't mean you have to move mountains. The attempt to take the first step not to play small, to live in your truth, to follow your dreams or not to hide is a success within itself, no matter how small or big you think the dream is or what the outcome may be.

CHAPTER 5 NOTES

- **What is the one passion, hobby, dream you've wanted to pursue but still haven't?** List one or as many as you like. Don't censor yourself. It doesn't matter how big, small, silly or crazy you think they may be. Don't let age or financial cost prevent you from listing them down. Remember, God has ways of opening doors for us that we couldn't even imagine.

_____

_____

_____

_____

- **What's the first step you can responsibly take in pursuing this passion, goal, hobby or dream?** Do you need to sign up for a course? Do you need to sit down with someone who is knowledgeable about what you're pursuing and get more info? Take the first step, even if you're scared, nervous or have butterflies in your stomach. Try not to over-think this too much. We're just talking about taking the first step here.

_____

_____

_____

_____

- **How would it feel to NEVER have tried to pursue this passion or interest of yours?**

_____
_____
_____
_____

"Self-care is not selfish or self-indulgent. We cannot nurture others from a dry well. We need to take care of our needs first, then we can give from our surplus, our abundance."
— JENNIFER LOUDEN

CHAPTER 6
Be Kind to Yourself

How can you give 100% in all areas of your life if you are not showing up 100% for yourself? The way you treat yourself will reflect in how successful and fulfilling the different areas of your life are. If you're not making yourself a priority by taking care of your needs, then your relationships with family, loved ones, friends, and co-workers will suffer. The way you treat yourself will impact the way you view others and life as a whole. I believe in order to fully cherish life and others, you need to love and respect yourself first. It's not enough to just say, "I love myself." You have to prove it to yourself by taking the loving actions necessary to take care of your needs.

I spoke a lot about spirituality, but the physical, mental, and emotional needs are important as well. Feeding your mind, body, and soul with the proper fuel is paramount in living a full, rich life. Taking care of yourself helps you live a healthier and happier life. How you treat your body ultimately affects your confidence and self-esteem, which in turn affects your relationships, be it professional or personal. We all owe it to ourselves to be kind to ourselves before we can dish any kindness into the world. Charity, as they say, begins at home.

After being diagnosed with ulcerative colitis in my teenage years (an autoimmune illness that affects the digestive system) and spending years on different medications and trying to find dietary balance to overcome this painful autoimmune disease, I finally took matters of my health and treatment into my own hands when I was in my late twenties. Conventional treatments for ulcerative colitis alone were not working to keep painful symptoms at bay; healing became a matter of life and death. I researched foods and supplements that would heal my body holistically.

Healing myself through nutrition was one of the methods that brought miraculous changes in my physical health. My health not only improved but I had a surge of energy that I hadn't felt before. It was then I realized that you are not only what you eat but what your body can absorb. I experienced firsthand the power and benefit of tailoring a diet that met my specific needs. I felt a duty to share this with the world, and this is one of the reasons why I went on to get my certification in health coaching.

Food can affect how good or crappy you feel emotionally. This can be subtle. There is something called the brain-gut connection. The vagus nerve is the longest of all our cranial nerves, and it creates a direct connection between our brain and our gut. The gut contains a chemical substance called serotonin. Serotonin is important for the functions of your brain and plays a key role in your mood and well-being. People call it the "feel good" chemical. Our gut creates 95% of that "feel good" chemical. Once I learned about the connection between the gut and brain, it started to make sense. Before making the switch to a healthier lifestyle, I battled with my mood being always up and down.

I always tell people that when my diet is clean, I'm an entirely different person than I am when my diet is not healthy. When I say clean diet, I mean the best type of food that is most loving and nourishing to MY body. As a health coach, I know that you are not only what you eat but what your body can absorb and process. We are all different, so we all have different nutrition requirements. Looking at my food and eating habits has been essential in my self-care. If I eat bad, I feel bad, my mood is not too pleasant, and I'm not my best self. I also need to be mindful of not going to the extreme. Eating healthy does not mean obsessively worrying about every morsel of food I put in my mouth. Food is nourishing and tasty. It's something I enjoy, but it is not meant to be a form of therapy. I see food differently. Its job is to fuel and sustain me, unlike before when I binged and used it as a medium of escape.

Another self-care routine that has been a life saver for me is exercise. I personally love how strength training feels but I think movements like taking long walks, yoga or even dancing can help with making your body and mind stronger and healthier and will help clear the clutter in your mind. For me, exercise was one of the first ways I was able to shut my mind off and breathe. I was able to shut the noise in the world out for that period of time. Exercise makes me feel calmer and loosens up the tightness and kinks from a busy and sometimes challenging day. I like the way my body looks as a result of exercising. I appreciate the transformation my body makes when I stick to an exercise routine. Exercise for me has to be enjoyable and loving, and although the physical benefits are amazing, it can't be all about squeezing into a certain pant size or having the scale tip a certain way. There is nothing wrong with wanting to look good and feeling beautiful and comfortable in your skin. Exercise and movement do help tremendously with that. However, exercise for me first and foremost is about releasing anything that's weighing me down.

Eating right and exercise were not enough; I had to make time to play, have fun and do things that brought me joy and made my heart smile. Playing and having fun had been so foreign to me. Once I embarked on my journey of self-improvement, I became so consumed with working hard to do better and be a better person that I forgot that fun and play had to be a part of the equation. I then made it a point to schedule time in my calendar for fun. Sometimes this would mean blocking out a few hours a week just to spend time with family and friends. The following week I would block out two hours and catch a movie or see live theater after work. I took salsa lessons for a bit.

Taking a warm bubble bath while reading a book brought me joy. I started getting manicures and pedicures just because, and not because of a special occasion. I'd splurge on mini massages. From time to time I'd wear nice outfits and heels to work instead of throwing on my same old pair of slacks and flats. These are things I had to pencil in because self-care and having fun were difficult at first. It just wasn't second nature. I had spent some years of my life inadvertently destroying it that when I finally started to pick up the pieces, it felt weird to carve out time for myself because I became so accustomed to working hard to fix and rebuild that I forgot to chill out and play.

The more I practice self-care, the more my self-esteem and self-worth increase. No guilt should be felt in putting yourself first. The way you care for yourself is how you will nourish the care you put into others. Life is meant to be enjoyed and not just endured. You're worthy of being a bit self-indulgent. You're not taking anything away from anyone. Self-care is a form of kindness and compassion towards yourself. And you have to be kind to yourself because no one else will do it for you. How kind we are to ourselves will mirror how kind we are to others and will also influence the way people around us treat us.

Indulge yourself in activities that make you feel good but are not self-sabotaging. Surround yourself with positive people who share your interests and with whom you can have a good laugh. Taking care of yourself also means not isolating yourself. Life is best lived in the company of good people. Take care of your emotional self and your attitude. Let it be positive towards you and others. And if you need help achieving this, you can get help through therapy. There is no shame in taking care of your emotional health. If there's no shame in going to the dentist to take care of your teeth, there should be no shame in going to see a psychologist to take care of your mind. Your mind is your most powerful tool; it is essential that you take care of it.

Eat healthy. Your body matters. What you eat determines the energy you put out. Don't mainly stuff junk into your body and expect to perform at an optimal level. Also, move daily. You don't have to take the elevator if you are not running late; try taking the stairs instead. Do cardio, a dance class, yoga, a long walk or any exercise, and you'd be amazed at how good this will make you feel. Be consistently kind to your body, and it will be kind to you in return. Wake up each morning, and promise yourself this: I will be kind to myself and treat my body like a temple.

CHAPTER 6 NOTES

- **What are some ways you can begin or continue taking care of yourself?** Think of ways to be a bit more self-indulgent. You absolutely need to and deserve to be. Think of what would possibly nourish your mind, body and soul. What would be fun? Don't be afraid to be daring or to think outside of the box.

_____
_____
_____
_____
_____
_____
_____
_____

"Be thankful for what you have; you'll end up having more. If you concentrate on what you don't have, you'll never, ever have enough."
— OPRAH WINFREY

CHAPTER 7
A Disease of More

Dr. Robert Emmons, who has been studying gratitude for many years and is considered by many to be the world's leading authority on gratitude, wrote a book on gratitude. In one of his research experiments, he explains that those who practice gratitude tend to deal with adversity better, have stronger immune systems, and stronger relationships than those who don't practice gratitude. We've all heard the saying, "Be grateful for what you have," many times in our lives. I think the topic of gratitude is so popular because although the idea sounds great, many of us fall short in this area or have a false sense of gratitude, meaning that gratitude is dependent on how great our lives are going.

It's easy to have gratitude when everything in your life is running smoothly. How does one practice gratitude in the midst of things like discomfort, uncertainty, pain, sorrow, and difficult circumstances? Gratitude when things aren't going right gives us perspective. It shows us light in the worst darkness. Gratitude helps us heal when we are broken, and when we despair, it has the power to bring us hope. Gratitude helps us cope no matter the situation we face and it is a practice we all need to make a habit of.

    I believe that one's outlook in life is a reflection of what's happening on the inside. When I was finally able to overcome my destructive behaviors and was on the path to becoming a better, less broken human being, a dear friend Laura told me that she felt that one of the root causes of my destructive behaviors and discontent was not the things that I used to escape with like food, cigarettes or alcohol but my disease of "more." I looked at her like she had grown three heads when she said this. I had no clue what she was referring to. She explained that I had a disease of "more," meaning I constantly wanted more of everything, and nothing was ever enough for me. Even after I overcame my toxic behaviors, she said the disease of more was still with me. She also told me that one of the ways to cure this disease of always wanting more and never being satisfied is through GRATITUDE.

I was completely livid when she told me this. Did she not see the work that I did on myself? The transformation I had made? I had the right to want more and better for myself. I had a right to go after more money, a bigger apartment, a better career, and a better neighborhood. What's wrong with wanting more? She said there was nothing wrong with my ambition to want more out of life, especially when it came to material things. Enjoying the fruits of my labor was perfectly fine, but she said that she noticed that I tend to complain a lot. I focused too much on what I didn't have.

This threw me for a loop because I had no clue that was the energy I was putting out to the universe. The truth was that she was somewhat right. I had been through hell and back and found myself slowly getting back on top, but that attitude of gratitude wasn't always present. I was constantly in "what's next" mode. The strides I had made on my journey of healing weren't enough. I could never appreciate what I had because I was constantly in a space of "I should be doing more," "Why don't I still have this?" "If only I didn't waste all those years cleaning up my life, I would've been further along in my career." I had food to eat, a few bucks in the bank, my health was fine, I had a family who loved and supported me, but there was that feeling of "That's it? This can't be it." There is nothing wrong with wanting more, but unfortunately, the problem was that I wasn't fully enjoying the things I was already blessed with. I wasn't completely content with the blessings that I had; instead, I was more focused on what I was lacking.

If someone asked me if I was grateful, I would, of course, say YES. Who would ever say no to a question like that? But most of the time, at my core, I didn't feel truly grateful. I was more indifferent to my blessings.

It was like any other normal weekday. I was at work when I got the call from my mom that my younger sister's results came back from the doctor's office and she was diagnosed with breast cancer. My body felt numb. The news hadn't registered. I stepped away from my desk, and I remember trying to calm my mother down over the phone while at work. When I got home that day, my sister's diagnosis started to sink in, but I didn't allow myself to feel any kind of pity, anger, heaviness or negative feelings. I just went into survival mode and put on my big sister/caretaker hat and devised a plan with my mom on the next steps to help my little sister.

Well, when it rains, it pours. A few weeks after my sister's diagnoses, my boss pulled me into her office and said I was being let go. The company wasn't doing well, and they had to go through a series of layoffs, and I was one of the first people to go. So now I had a sister with cancer I had to tend to and no job. I went on interviews, but nothing was promising. I lived in an expensive city with bills to pay and a depleting savings account. Although I wasn't allowing myself to let the negative feelings in, my body felt the stress that I was under. My ulcerative colitis that had been in remission started to rear its ugly head (a big trigger for any autoimmune illness is stress). My life at that particular point felt unmanageable. I was running on adrenaline.

A few weeks later, my sister started chemo, and her health looked like it was getting worst. She lost all her hair and she was bloated because of all the chemicals they were pumping into her. She looked frail and at times looked like death. But there was one moment I'll never forget: I was sitting with my sister by her bedside during one of her chemo treatments, and I remember her taking "selfies" and posting her journey on Facebook. She was a fighter and an inspiration to the people around her. I thought to myself, if I was in that position, the last thing

I'd want to do was post selfies, fight and be an inspiration to anybody.

That day for some reason, I was calm and quiet enough to examine her demeanor and interactions with family members that came to visit, as well as the hospital staff. It was in that moment, I finally learned and understood what it meant to be grateful. She didn't have a bitter bone in her body; she was still very pleasant despite her diagnosis, pain, suffering, and uncertainty about how things would end up. She was living life in the moment. And in that moment she was alive, getting treatment and appreciating the help she was getting. She was full of hope and light. She had so much gratitude. I was completely amazed and moved by my sister, but at the same time, I was embarrassed for myself that I wasn't someone who was naturally grateful.

I went home that afternoon and sat on my floor and wept. I cried for a long time. I cried for my sister; I cried at the thought of possibly losing her. I cried that I didn't know how I would support myself financially. I cried out of the frustration of not taking care of myself and giving room for my symptoms from my digestive illness to creep back in. All the feelings I suppressed during that time period came tumbling down. The fear crept in and the self-pity waltzed right in, but this time I allowed myself to have these feelings with no judgments. I took a deep breath, pulled out a piece of paper and began to write a gratitude list. It was an act that wasn't foreign to me but one I hadn't done in a very long time. I was in my head too much, and I needed to be able to write and have something tangible to look at. Although things seemed bleak at the time, I was able to see clearly how God was carrying my family and me, taking care of my important needs.

I realized that what we have and the world as we know it can be taken away from us in a blink of an eye. At that moment, I felt a surge of gratitude for the fact that my sister had a great medical staff taking care of her. I felt grateful that since I wasn't working at the time, I was able to go to chemo treatments with her. I felt grateful for my unemployment check, I felt grateful that rent was paid for the month and I had enough money to feed myself for the week. I felt a new level of humility.

By the special grace of God, my sister beat cancer, and I got back on my feet and was blessed with a better job than the one I had. My sister was my greatest teacher in the lesson of gratitude. Gratitude is something I try to practice daily. For a long time, gratitude wasn't second nature. When the voice in my head wants to complain about what I don't have or live in a place of "want, want, want," I quickly take out a note pad, or if there is no pad, I'll use the notes section on my phone and write a quick gratitude list. The good thing is, with technology, there is no excuse not to jot down what I'm grateful for. Or if for some reason the list is not enough, I pray a simple prayer: "Dear, God, thank you, and just for today, help me to want what I have."

I remind myself I'm right where I need to be. I am enough, and I have enough. I also know that what you put out into the universe is what you'll receive. So if I think in abundance, the universe will continue to add to my life. If I send out a signal to the universe that I don't have enough and I'm unhappy with what I have, then the universe will keep subtracting from what I have. Staying in gratitude doesn't mean you deny the challenges of a particular circumstance in your life; it just means you're shifting your focus and seeing the glass as half full instead of half empty.

CHAPTER 7 NOTES

Gratitude is a muscle I had to build. It didn't come naturally for me. Many times, I had to remind myself of WHY practicing gratitude was essential. I had to remind myself of the benefits I would receive: increased energy, increased contentment and optimism, less anxiety and worry, a more pleasant attitude, decreased stress, reduced feelings of envy, better health and immune system, etc.

Eventually, gratitude wasn't just in my head; it was in my heart. Doing a gratitude list has proven to be a great reset button when I'm having a bad day.

- **List at least 5 things you are grateful for and WHY you are grateful for them.**

The **WHY** is the most **IMPORTANT**. I've come to realize that knowing my WHY helps to deepen my appreciation for what I have. Of course, you can put more than 5. The more you put gratitude into practice, the more the list increases and the easier this exercise gets. You can literally do this exercise almost anywhere and at any time of the day.

_____
_____
_____
_____
_____

"Call it a clan, call it a network, call it a tribe, call it a family. Whatever you call it, whoever you are, you need one."
— Jane Howard

CHAPTER 8
The Inner Circle

It's essential to have a tribe or a circle of people that share similar interests, beliefs, and or values, a group of people who will support you and have your back. A circle of people that want to see you uplifted and successful in all areas of your life. When I made the decision to do better in my life, I started to attract people along the way that uplifted me and wanted to see me win. It's impossible for any of us to go through this adventure called life alone. These people believed in me when I didn't believe in myself. They loved me when at times I didn't love myself. I have individuals in my life I can turn to when I need sound advice, an ear to vent to, people I can brainstorm with or just pray with. I am also that person they can ask for help, collaborate with, and lean on.

Finding people you are aligned with makes the road less rocky. It fills you with a sense of assurance and makes you generally more confident about life. Life definitively gets easier when you know you have people you can lean on, a set of shoulders to cry on should you need one, and people who are always rooting for you. Life can be tough and it's best when we do not walk it alone. We need people we can share our joy with, our sadness, our frustrations and people who we can equally be there for. These are people who make life a whole lot more beautiful.

Sharon and Charles were great friends of mine whom I loved and cherished dearly. We were three peas in a pod. We spent every other day together after work and a huge amount of time on the weekends. I noticed when I started to make changes in my life they had a lot of questions, which I totally understood. These were the friends that I would hang out with, party all night, get drunk and smoke with. They didn't understand why I wanted to stop doing those things. I explained to them that it was no longer serving me and it was no longer fun. These activities were causing me more harm than good. They said they thought I was overreacting. I assured them that I wasn't, and although I no longer wanted to participate in those activities, it didn't mean that I didn't want them in my life. Surely, there were other activities that we could do, and we did. We all knew each other's families and were quite close, and this for me meant that we had a lot in common and we had strong bonds. I was open to any activity that wasn't detrimental to my well-being.

But something happened. Now that we weren't in our usual environments, the conversations, small talk, and the rapport was different. We didn't have much to talk about. Conversations were shorter and we butted heads on things we normally wouldn't butt heads on. Sharon and Charles thought that my desire to have a different life than the one before was a little over the top. Even though I still wanted them in my life, we soon learned that we actually didn't have much in common as we had thought. I didn't want to let them go despite it, but the fact was, they were pulling away. They invited me out less and the calls from them were few and far between. Then came the blow to my heart. Sharon and Charles just stopped returning my calls, and I didn't understand why. After weeks of trying to hunt them down, Charles finally gave me a call and said they thought it would be best if I did my "own thing."

Both Charles and Sharon thought I was walking around thinking I was better than everyone. I was devastated for weeks following that call. I was also angry at them. I called them every dirty name in the book, in my head of course. I was angry that they wouldn't support the better and improved me. Why did they take me trying to heal as me being better than them? Couldn't they see that was never my intention? If they loved me, why didn't they understand that? I had no choice but to respect their wishes and part ways, but I held a resentment against them for a long time.

Thank goodness I had people in my life who were able to point me in the right direction and help me get over the resentment I had for Sharon and Charles. As my transformation started to take shape, I noticed that a few more people I considered friends were no longer there for me. In hindsight, I realize that those few people who turned their backs on me or drifted away weren't bad people. The part they played in my story was just over. Coming to that conclusion was painful. You will have a core group of people who will be with you from beginning to end. There will also be people who won't care enough to be around you as you change, and you will have to accept that this is okay too. They won't appreciate your transformation, ambition or understand your new needs and desires, so they will push you away or slowly fade from your life. Your choices and new life will not be aligned with their life, and vice versa. They will have no desire to get to know or support the new you no matter how fabulous you think the new you has become. I was no better or less than them; we just wanted different things out of life, and whatever held us connected before was broken for whatever reason. There's a reason for the saying "Birds of a feather flock together."

It was explained to me that having a network of likeminded people was essential. Although I have a core group of friends and family who are always by my side, it was also necessary to find people who were on the same path as I was—a group of people who shared similar interests, beliefs, and values, a group of people I could turn to for matters relating to career, success, spirituality, and everyday life matters, a tribe I could lean on and be comfortable exposing my vulnerabilities to.

I call myself an extroverted introvert. People usually think I'm more extroverted than I really am. Don't get me wrong, I love people and I'm a people person. Once I started to love myself, my compassion and desire to get closer to others increased. Now, I truly like to get to know others, and not just on a surface level. When I ask someone how they are, it's not to fill air but to truly find out how they are doing. But I'm also a big introvert, and my default setting is to isolate from others and not let people in. I don't care to show my vulnerabilities and weaknesses to others. I would much rather solve my problems and issues alone. If I'm experiencing challenges with a particular issue or person, no matter how big or small, I write, pray or meditate over it. These are all good things, but I realize that I didn't get to be the woman I am today all alone. I know there is a part of me that likes to isolate and lay low, so I make it a point not to hide and withdraw from people too much. People were placed in my life to guide me directly and indirectly. Thinking I don't need anyone's help or support is the worst disservice I can do for myself.

I had to start getting out of my comfort zone and placing myself in settings that attracted the people who inspired me. I wanted to be around people who would cause me to say, "I want what they have." Not what they had physically or materially, but how their light shined as they walked in a room—their ambition, their drive, their understanding, love, and empathy for other people. This meant I had to try new things, like going to different social events, venues, and outings I normally wouldn't go to. It meant meeting people who were perhaps different from me and of a different race, socio-economic background, etc., but who shared a similar vision in terms of what we wanted out of life. Finding my tribe really helped to break the monotony of my life as well. My life would feel so empty without my tribe.

Your tribe, soul family, network, crew, whatever you want to call it are there to not only help uplift, encourage, guide and cheer you on, but also to be honest. We can't escape the fact that we're all flawed human beings. This is what makes us dynamic, unique and interesting, but sometimes a few of our flaws or mistakes can hinder our opportunity for growth personally and professionally. Having someone who will call you out on your stuff is also a role that someone in your tribe should play. We're going to fall short, and the people around you will respect and care enough about you to let you know when you mess up, whether you want to hear it or not. You need that one person in your crew to keep you level-headed.

The people in my tribe play different roles. Some are amazing when it comes to business and career. Others help me grow spiritually. Others are there to be with me when I need to let loose and forget about any worries from my day, week or the world. A few are there when I need a shoulder to cry on. Sometimes, they have no advice to offer but just their ear to listen, arms to hold me, and shoulders to lean on. I believe we attract the people we are or are becoming. It feels good to be at a place where I have a tribe of people who will look out for me and ones I will take care of and look out for as well.

The purpose of a network or tribe is not to take, take, and take. It can't be a one-way street. There is strength and power in numbers. Finding your tribe may take a little bit of time, especially if you're still trying to find what your needs, hopes, goals, and desires are, but you will see that some of the members of your tribe will find you. You'll be at the right place at the right time. Stay humble, positive, open and willing to receive your tribe. They may come in ways you least expect, such as at your favorite book club, a networking event or a religious gathering, or they may be older, younger, more successful or less, and none of these will matter when you meet them. Your souls will connect at the purest level devoid of all pretense because you share the same values, interests, desires, and slowly a goal will unite you all: the goal to be there for each other, no matter what life throws at you.

CHAPTER 8 NOTES

*"You are the average of the five people
you spend the most time with."*
– JIM ROHN

- **What are the names of the people who make up your tribe?**

These are the people you would turn to regarding career, family, spirituality, emotional support, etc. You might only be able to turn to certain members of your tribe regarding one area of your life, and that's perfectly fine. Not everyone will be equipped or have the tools to support you in all areas. Every member of your tribe will have their own strengths and weaknesses. But they will all have one desire in common and that is to see you WIN and THRIVE.

_____

_____

_____

_____

- **If you're in the process of finding a tribe, then where are some places you can start meeting people who share similar interests, beliefs and vision as you?** Examples: Meet-up groups, in-person and online community groups, churches, spiritual centers, events and summits, etc.

_____
_____
_____
_____

- **Who in your life is mentally, spiritually and emotionally draining or bringing negativity to your life?**

Think about the ones who are back stabbers, who have a bad attitude, who constantly talk negatively, and who seem to take but never give. These are the people you will need to eventually ditch or love at a distance.

_____
_____
_____
_____

"At the end of the day it's not about what you have or even what you've accomplished. It's about who you've lifted up, who you've made better. It's about what you've given back."
— DENZEL WASHINGTON

CHAPTER 9
Being of Service

I've heard people say that a life where you are not giving back is a life not worth living. I used to think this was a bit dramatic. I now realize the importance of giving back. The feelings I get from giving back are sometimes priceless. You're not only making a positive impact in the world or on the people around you, but the intangible benefits you receive enhance your life. At the end of the day, your journey will not be fulfilling if the only focus is SELF. What I didn't know about service then and I've since found out is that you don't have to move mountains to make a difference in other people's lives. A few small acts of kindness and service can be profound. I also realized that the definition of being of service went beyond what I actually thought service was.

I have volunteered with individuals who were wheelchair-bound. My job was to help them with physical exercise activities to keep them well and strong. I have taken my nutrition skills and education to assist in preparing and serving food at women's shelters. I've mentored middle school students with resume writing. I have also volunteered my time at various food pantries. I was able to see firsthand some of the resources that were lacking in the communities I worked in. I was able to see the holes and the gaps and was able to have an idea of how my services, education, knowledge, and background could help fill those gaps. The people that I volunteered my services to were some of the most amazing and beautiful human beings I've ever met.

I grew up in an underserved and sometimes forgotten community, so giving back was always of the utmost importance to me. The people I usually help are almost always so kind and filled with gratitude. It was easy to give of myself. My definition of service has expanded; it doesn't only include supporting the less fortunate. Being of service now has to be integrated into every part of my life. The way I live in this world and the way I treat others is the main indicator of how well I'm doing. I've also now realized that being of service can happen in the littlest of ways, as little as how I choose to react to people and circumstances around me.

I live in New York City, known to many as the Big Apple and the capital of the world. It's a place with rich cultures and diverse groups of people. We're known for our tough skin. We work hard and play even harder. We stand up for what's right. We fight for each other. With that said, NY is fast-paced. People always seem to be in a rush, sometimes appear to have a lot on their mind or look like they don't want to be bothered. This is especially true on the NYC subways, which is most people's main form of public transportation. Even if you own a car, it's sometimes easier to commute on the subways. It can be very convenient. I always say if you want to get a glimpse of what the characters of NY look like, hop on a subway ride for a few minutes. You will see all types of personalities, races, ages, socio-economic classes, sexual orientation, and the list goes on. The subway is a microcosm of New York City. Traveling on the subway during rush hour is probably one of the most tiresome challenges for New Yorkers, and I'm no exception. My morning and evening commutes can sometimes be filled with major subway delays, people yelling and arguing and people invading the little space I have while standing up or sitting down, if I'm even lucky to get a seat. Commuting on the subways is the least Zen place I will ever find myself.

I used to always get frustrated with the chaos of the subways, the rude people I sometimes encounter, the pushing and the shoving just to get on the subway on time. As soon as I step foot on the subway during rush hour, my chest gets tight, my body gets tense, my breathing becomes a little heavier, and I'm not as calm. I'm also almost always agitated and rolling my eyes (in my head of course). My face says it all. This is usually my default reaction. Many times I can't help my default reaction, but I have the opportunity and the responsibility to change it. Negative energy attracts negative energy. If I have negative energy, all I will see or take in is negativity. I will block anybody's good energy out. While on the subway, I ask myself how I can be of service amidst this chaotic commute. Yes, being of service is as small as how am I reacting to the people on the subway around me. How is my demeanor? How is my energy?

If I have a frown on my face and I feel frustrated, I immediately take a moment to look at something or someone on the subway who will turn my frown into a smile. I smile at my fellow passenger. Or maybe gaze at the fun little baby in her baby carriage. If I find myself getting in my head, lashing out at people in my head, and being judgmental of the people crowded around me, I immediately switch gears and try to think of one positive thing about those strangers on the train; it can be a garment they are wearing that's beautiful or striking; maybe they have great hair or a great pair of shoes. I try to humanize them in my head. If I see someone acting rude or mean on the train, I actually try to pray for them because only wounded and hurt people treat people badly. Having this mind shift is being of service.

Being of service doesn't stop there. It spills into your interactions with people in the other areas of your life. How am I treating my co-workers? Am I being kind? Am I participating in office gossip directly or indirectly? Am I putting my fair share into my work? When I go to the coffee shop to get my morning coffee, I make sure I smile and ask the barista how he or she is doing. Their attitude, whether good or bad, should have no impact on my gentleness towards them. I'm reminded that something as small as a smile to a stranger as you walk pass them in the street is being of service. Letting the driver who's driving next to you get ahead of you is being of service. Almost any action where you're thinking of the other people is being of service. I'm human, and I will sometimes slip into ME, ME, ME, mode. What do I want? What do I need? What don't I have?

Being of service especially helps when I find myself slipping into this mode. When I see myself going there, I ask myself, "Who can I be of service to right now?" The answer can be as simple as picking up the phone and calling a friend or relative and seeing how they're doing and if they need anything. Put your focus on someone other than yourself for that moment. Or maybe it can be writing a letter to your congressman or state assemblyman to voice your opinions on what is needed to make a difference in your community. Make your focus about looking out for someone at that moment.

The key is to be of service without expecting anything in return, but the secret is that you get everything in return: peace of mind, a positive mindset, and a good feeling knowing that you are helping increase the positive vibration in this world. Being of service is a great solution when you find yourself being self-absorbed, focusing on things that stress you out. When I'm in a place of turmoil, distress, and pain, being of service and trying to uplift at least one person around me has sometimes proved to be the most helpful. Service increases my optimism. There are times I may not be in the right headspace, my attitude is not great, and I have no desire to be of service; those are the times I actually need to be of service even more. When I find myself in that space, I pray for a few seconds and ask for guidance. I ask God to help me be of service and to use me. Believe it or not, I sometimes think I get more out of the act of being of service than the recipient I'm of service to. There are not too many people who can say that their lives haven't been enriched by giving back and being of service.

CHAPTER 9 NOTES

- **List at least 3-5 ways you can be of service in the upcoming week.**

Examples of being of service: Volunteering at a soup kitchen; calling a dear friend you haven't checked up on in a while; lending an ear to someone who is going through a hard time; offering to babysit for a friend, a couple or loved one who could use some alone time; or asking a co-worker, who is struggling with their workload, if they need help. The opportunities to be of service are endless. You don't have to find the cure to cancer to be of service. No act of kindness is too small.

_____

_____

_____

_____

_____

"The more you take personal responsibility for your actions and behaviors, the freer you'll be."
— JOANE CAJUSTE

CHAPTER 10
It's not about them

As I continued to clean house and repair the parts of my life that were cracked, I started to finally become comfortable knowing that I am an imperfect human being and my actions and behaviors will no doubt prove that. I am no longer comfortable with unsavory behavior or actions from myself. I know better now. As I begin to grow into the person I'm meant to be, I must continually take inventory of my actions and behavior on a daily basis. This is not a form of punishment but a way of freeing myself and releasing anything that keeps my mind, spirit or heart in shackles. I must take ownership when I've wronged someone or made a mistake. It's my responsibility now to continually check in with myself and see if I'm harboring negative emotions such as bitterness, jealousy, envy, pride, resentment, or greed. This task seemed daunting at first, but it was necessary in order for me to not revert to the old Joane: unhappy, insecure, depressed, resentful, fearful, pointing the finger, and putting the blame on others. I operate differently now, and when I find myself sliding back to the old, wounded Joane, the action of daily self-reflection is a healthy dose of reality.

I am deeply affected and saddened by the political climate we are living in, as most of us are. It doesn't matter what side of the political spectrum we are on; most of us are going through a series of emotions on a daily basis when it comes to our world and our liberties, such as fear, frustration, anger, sometimes hope and hopelessness. I am no exception. Politics divide people and tear people apart. People lash out at each other, judge each other, call each other names, and point the finger. I have my own political beliefs, and when someone doesn't see my point of view, it can sometimes make me sad and frustrated. I find myself judging them, disregarding, ignoring or even at times disliking them, especially if I think they're coming from a place of hate. There is not much room for those feelings of hatred and judgments in my life. I can't help when they arise, but when they do, it's my job to do my best to release those feelings that bring me further away from becoming the woman I am meant to be.

A way I clean house and get rid of the unwanted feelings is admitting what I'm feeling, how it's hurting me, see how those feelings are not benefiting me and examine what I can do to change them. I typically will do this type of process or homework with someone I trust, like an accountability partner, one with whom I can share my resentments and judgments with. We come up with ways I can release them. Sometimes the answer may mean putting myself in the shoes of the person I am harboring negative feelings towards. I imagine what they're thinking, why they're thinking that and what could possibly be some of their fears and concerns. Sometimes, it's not about whether the person is actually mean, hateful or nice, but about looking solely on the part I play and looking at my own reactions. This process for me is typically done on a daily basis. My accountability partner, Marsha, and I call it our check-in time.

Our check-in time is where we check in with each other regarding our well-being and discuss any negative feelings we are harboring or dissect any emotions that are eating away at us. This process doesn't have to take long. I can go through periods where I'm not taking this action, but I try never to go days or weeks where the negative feelings or emotions linger in my spirit without turning it over to a trusted source. Another example in my life where this type of house cleaning is necessary can be as simple as putting someone down directly or indirectly. I'm not one to go around hurting people on purpose, but there have been times where I get into compare-and-despair mode, meaning I slip into the old habit of focusing on the abundance that others have and comparing my abundance to theirs. When I'm not centered and grounded, I can still easily fall into the space of feeling insecure and jealous, and in my head, I'll make a slick remark about the other person.

The mere thought of comparison is harmful. Some people even call it criminal. I have my big girl panties on, so I now can admit to myself when those feelings of fear, jealousy, and envy come up. The light in me will not let me ignore those feelings and sweep them under the rug. I feel those feelings as if they were a knot in the pit of my stomach, in my chest, and in my throat. So I take action to rid myself of those toxic feelings and unsavory mental thinking. I check in with my accountability partner Marsha again, sometimes at the end of the day, or I'll step away from whatever I'm doing, go to a quiet place and open up to my accountability buddy. I may or may not go into details about the person I'm harboring ill emotions against, but I'll discuss the feelings I'm having, and then we come up with a quick plan of attack. Sometimes, I'll journal about it for a few minutes; write about why I feel this way, and what I am threatened by. What am I fearful of? I pray for peace and blessings for the person and even more abundance for them. I then rip or shred the pages up and throw them away. The act of writing it helps unload the dead weight.

Last but not the least, there are those actions and behaviors that may require me to apologize directly to an individual. As long as my apology will not cause any harm or unnecessary damage, it's imperative I address the individual sooner than later. We all know when we've slighted someone or done something wrong to someone. We get to a place when our conscience speaks to us. No matter how small the wrong is, I do my best to apologize. This can be anywhere from how I speak to someone, the tone of voice, my demeanor, my attitude, showing up late somewhere or just not showing up and honoring my commitment to something. I make amends and try to turn things around if I can. If I can't find the right words to form an apology, I seek guidance. I have mentors, spiritual leaders, my network/tribe, and trusted sources I can now turn to if I need help humbling myself to take the necessary action in apologizing and making amends. I don't obsess over every behavior because I don't think that would be a loving act towards myself. The goal here is not to live life tallying up everything I'm doing wrong but to address those few behaviors and acts that interfere with my spiritual, mental, and emotional growth. I know when it's time to take a step back and put myself in check.

One of the most life changing questions I heard someone ask one day was, "How free do you want to be?" So, I pose the same question to you. If the answer is as free as possible, then taking inventory of your actions, behaviors, and motives as often as possible is one of your many paths to freedom. This act of introspection is not meant to beat ourselves up. This process keeps us on our toes in continuing to lead an honest life, non-manipulative, and kind life. The more we practice this action, the less we will find ourselves having to apologize, making amends or cleaning house. We get better at anticipating and recognizing when the negative behavior and emotions are stirring up, and we can nip them in the bud right away. We have to realize that the bulk of the work lies with us. We cannot control other people's actions, but we can control ours and our reactions to them.

We can decide to let toxic things go, we can choose to be happy, and we can choose to be free in the constant act of reflection. You can get your own accountability partner, someone who believes in the same set of values as you do and wants happiness and freedom for you. It may be your spouse, or a friend, someone who helps you keep your actions and emotions in check, and you do the same for them. It is with this effort of constant reflection that we do our best to live an honest, non-manipulative, heart-centered, positive and freer life.

So how free do you want to be?

CHAPTER 10 NOTES

Taking a moment at the end of the day to reflect on what has gone well, and where things may have gone wrong, is one of the keys to success and fulfillment. This self-reflection is necessary for personal and professional growth. This action makes us stronger, more peaceful, and more productive.

A lack of self-awareness can hinder our goals and our relationship with ourselves and others. We must continue to take responsibility for our OWN actions and behaviors. This daily exercise can be done at the end of the day or anytime during the day.

- **Make a list of all the things that went well TODAY. List things that you did that you felt good about and things you've accomplished.**

_____

_____

_____

- **Jot down anything that went wrong today and what you can improve on.** Examples: People you came across that you may have slighted, things you might have dropped the ball on, consider things like gossip about others and negative statements about individuals you may have made, commitments to others you didn't keep, being short-tempered, having bad attitude, etc.

___

Bad days are inevitable. It's great to have someone you can call and check in with, someone you feel safe with. You'll also be able to vent to this person. This person can serve as your accountability partner or accountability buddy.

When there is a right decision or right action you know that should be taken, your accountability partner or buddy may help hold you accountable or provide encouragement and support. (Please note: Your accountability partner is not a substitute for a counselor or therapist.)

- **Write down the names of one or two people you can check in with or call during the day when feelings of frustration, negativity, anger, animosity, judgment, and irritability creep in.**

___

The above exercise has helped me to PAUSE and take a step back when needed. It has kept me from doing or saying something I might have regretted. This exercise has increased my patience and compassion for myself and others.

> "A strange beautiful woman met me in the mirror the other night. Hey, I said, what you doing here? She asked me the same thing."
> — MARILYN NELSON

CONCLUSION

Sometimes all we need is a look in the mirror to really see ourselves as complete. I hope this book has been a mirror to you. I hope you know how important you are now and how you can go on to live a life God has designed for you to live. I hope you are aware that no matter the hurdles you are going through, you can overcome them.

You can leave behind the habits that disguise themselves as pleasure when all they really do is harm you. You can find comfort in the support of others. You can move on from disappointment with hope in your heart that something better will come along. And above all, you won't give up on yourself, just as God will never give up on you.

I like the woman I am becoming. I'm falling in love with the person I see in the mirror now. Every day I wake up, I'm thankful for her. The woman in the mirror is no longer the enemy, and that's one of the greatest truths I've come to embrace. I am my own best ally, and because of this, I treat myself accordingly. I treat my mind, spirit, and body with the respect that they deserve, knowing there's no substitute for them.

I'm better equipped at loosening my grip when I find myself trying to hold on so tight for dear life now. I remember to breathe and let go of things that aren't mine to control in the first place. Whether I'm holding on to a person, idea, thought or situation. I'm learning to surrender to things that are out of my control because I know it is okay not to have everything under control. Yes, it is okay; just breathe.

Letting go of things is easier when you know you've got God, and I cannot over emphasize this. I'm very conscious of this fact. I feel God in me and around me. I make sure my spiritual connection is solid at all times. We all need something outside of ourselves to be tethered to. I make sure to listen when He speaks and watch out for Him speaking in the many forms with which He does.

I have also now acquired the tools to pause before reacting. Many of them I have shared in this book, and I hope you will make use of them. As humans, we grow every day one way or the other. We either grow in wisdom or in ignorance. The difference between these two is how we react to the everyday stimulus around us. I think growth is the pause button between thinking and reaction.

I try my best to pause and think before I do anything. I know that even with all the many situations and actions that surround me, which I do not have control over, I can at least decide how I react to them, and that gives me much power. I can pause and take a deep breath, think about the problem, and then react. I've realized how much good we can actually bring into the world when we pause, think, and then react. I hope you take time to pause and ponder over the content of this book as I have in many ways. Because of these lessons, I'm a better person.

Lastly, God is not done with me. He will keep waking me so that I can continue to fulfill my purpose in serving others and enriching other people's lives with the skills and gifts I have been given. I believe now more than ever that I'm meant to live a life of abundance, peace, and joy, no matter the whispers of negativity or self-doubt I may hear from time to time. And I know that the light I have within me gives me those things regardless of what the material world gives me.

How often do you look out for God around you, be it in nature or through meditation or even going for a religious gathering? Whatever your spiritual practice is, it is important that you keep at it. I make sure to hear God by allowing myself to listen. He speaks to me through various ways. Through spiritual books, meditation, as well as other people. How well do you hear God? If you aren't, maybe you've not taken the time to hear him above the loud noise of the hustle and bustle of this world.

God is not done with you! There are plans that he has for your life and a purpose that he has given you that only you can fulfill. With God, everything else becomes easier. You can pause to think before you react and you can loosen your grip on things that do not serve you, knowing there are better things ahead for you, because indeed there are.

Made in the USA
Middletown, DE
21 October 2017